CRAFTS FROM MANY CULTURES

FESTIVALS

Meryl Doney

Gareth Stevens Publishing
A WORLD ALMANAC EDUCATION GROUP COMPANY

About this Book

Each year, so many festivals are held around the world that one book cannot possibly mention them all. This book looks at some of the world's best-known festivals — as well as some of the most spectacular ones! The festivals featured come from different countries, cultures, and religions. Each left-hand page describes a festival as it is celebrated in one or more countries or continents. Full-color photographs are included to show some of the wonderful items related to the festival's celebrations. Each right-hand page provides step-by-step instructions, with illustrations, for making one of the festival items shown. You can try making these items either on your own or as group projects at school or with a club. The preparations and the time that goes into making things for celebrations are part of what makes any festival great. Have fun celebrating!

Most of the steps for making the projects in this book are easy to follow, but wherever you see this symbol, ask for help from an adult.

Measurement Conversions:

1 inch = 25.4 millimeters (mm)
1 inch = 2.54 centimeters (cm)
1 foot = 0.3048 meter (m)
1 yard = 0.9144 meter (m)
1 cup (8 ounces) liquid =
    240 milliliters (ml)
1 ounce dry weight = 28 grams (g)
    flour (1 cup = 5 ounces or 140g)
    salt (1 cup = 7 ounces or 196g)

Please visit our web site at: www.garethstevens.com
For a free color catalog describing Gareth Stevens Publishing's list of high-quality books and multimedia programs, call 1-800-542-2595 (USA) or 1-800-387-3178 (Canada). Gareth Stevens Publishing's fax: (414) 332-3567.

Library of Congress Cataloging-in-Publication Data

Doney, Meryl, 1942-
        Festivals / by Meryl Doney.
            p. cm. — (Crafts from many cultures)
        Includes bibliographical references and index.
        Summary: Introduces a variety of festivals and holidays from around the world and provides instructions for related crafts, including a dragon toy for the Chinese New Year, dancing wings for Mardi Gras, and a sugar skull for Halloween.
        ISBN 0-8368-4043-7 (lib. bdg.)
        1. Handicraft—Juvenile literature. 2. Festivals—Juvenile literature. [1. Festivals. 2. Holidays. 3. Handicraft.] I. Title.
TT160.D665   2004
745.594'1—dc22   2003055861

This North American edition first published in 2004 by
Gareth Stevens Publishing
A World Almanac Education Group Company
330 West Olive Street, Suite 100
Milwaukee, Wisconsin 53212 USA

First published as *World Crafts: Festivals* in 1995 by Franklin Watts, 96 Leonard Street, London WC2A 4XD, England. Additional end matter copyright © 2004 by Gareth Stevens, Inc.

Franklin Watts series editor: Kyla Barber
Franklin Watts editor: Jane Walker
Design: Visual Image
Artwork: Ruth Levy
Photography: Peter Millard

Additional photographs:
Christine Osborne Pictures: 20 (top); Forbes Magazine Collection, New York/Bridgeman Art Library, London: 12 (top); Robert Frerck/Odyssey, Chicago/Robert Harding Picture Library: 22 (top); Mary Evans Picture Library: 14 (top); Tony Morrison/South American Pictures: 8 (top); Peter Newark's Pictures: 16 (top).

Gareth Stevens editors: Dorothy L. Gibbs and JoAnn Early Macken
Gareth Stevens cover design: Kami Koenig

Very special thanks to Myra McDonnell, advisor and model maker.

Printed in the United States of America

1 2 3 4 5 6 7 8 9 08 07 06 05 04

Contents

A World of Festivals   4
Make a Festival Crafts Kit

Happy New Year! — China   6
Make a Chinese Dragon Toy

Mardi Gras — Brazil and Trinidad   8
Make Dancing Wings

The *Eid* festivals — Pakistan   10
Make an *Eid* Card

Easter — Germany, Ukraine, and Russia   12
Make a Fabergé-Style Egg

Welcoming Spring — India and Europe   14
Make a Green Man Mask

Honoring Ancestors — North America and China   16
Make Hell Bank Money

Everyday Faith — Russia, Italy, and Tibet   18
Make a Prayer Wheel

Harvest Festivals — Israel, United States, and United Kingdom   20
Make Harvest Paperweights

Halloween and All Souls' Day — North America and Mexico   22
Make a Sugar Skull

Founders' Days — Myanmar and India   24
Make a Portrait Garland

Festivals of Light — India and Israel   26
Make Diwali Lights

Christmas — India, Nigeria, and Peru   28
Make a Retablo Scene

Glossary   30

More Books to Read — Web Sites   31

Index   32

A World of Festivals

Festivals date back to the world's earliest times. Large fireplaces found inside caves suggest that prehistoric peoples gathered to eat and drink together, and it's not difficult to imagine that they also told stories, made music, sang, and danced.

People all over the world celebrate festivals. Most of the world's greatest festivals are religious in origin, and each one has its own customs, foods, and special rituals. Some religious festivals celebrate the birth of a religion's founder. Others honor memorable events in stories of faith.

Harvests have always been special times for festivals, too. Growing food is very important in most societies, and it takes many long, backbreaking hours of work. Reaping harvests and eating the food are times of joy and relaxation when the work is done.

Throughout history, people living in the world's temperate regions have been affected by changing seasons as Earth completes its yearly orbit around the Sun. Many people celebrate the seasons with festivals of light in the dark months and with dancing during lighter and warmer times of the year.

Activities that have been associated with some festivals for centuries are still important to many people in the world today. Celebrations include family and public gatherings, eating and drinking together, making and displaying special decorations, wearing special clothing and jewelry, and generally having fun. Sometimes, the festivities take weeks of preparation.

Make a Festival Crafts Kit

If you are planning to make some of the festival crafts in this book, you might want to put together a kit containing the most common tools and materials you will need. Here is a list of some supplies for your kit:

scissors • craft knife • hole punch • ruler • tape measure • newspaper • tracing paper • pencil • felt-tipped pen • colored markers •

chalk • acrylic paints • fabric paints • paintbrushes • clear tape • masking tape • glue • stapler and staples • safety pins • straight pins • needle and thread

Potato Dough

This dough recipe comes from one traditionally used in Peru for making retablos (see page 29), but it can also be used instead of modeling clay to make all kinds of figures. This dough does not have to be cooked, but it will dry very quickly if left uncovered.

You will need:
- **3 tablespoons instant mashed potato flakes**
- **10 tablespoons plaster of paris**
- **5 ounces boiling water**

In a small bowl, mix the potato flakes with the water. Stir with a spoon until smooth. In a larger bowl, mix the plaster of paris with 3 tablespoons of cold water. Stir until the plaster has a smooth, creamy texture. Combine the potato and plaster mixtures to form a dough, then knead the dough.

Salt Dough

You will need:
- **2 cups of flour**
- **¹/₂ cup of salt**
- **³/₄ cup of water**

In a large bowl, mix together the flour and the salt. Make a well in the middle of the mixture, then pour a little water into the well and stir it into the flour with a fork. Keep adding water, a little at a time, until you have used up all of the water.

When you have finished mixing in the water, knead the dough with your hands. If the dough is too sticky, add more flour. If it is too dry, add more water.

Salt dough must be dried in an oven to make it harden.

Happy New Year!

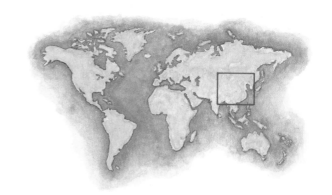

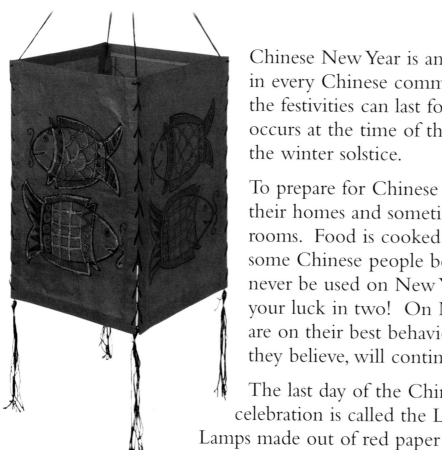

Chinese New Year is an important celebration in every Chinese community in the world, and the festivities can last for many days. This festival occurs at the time of the second new moon after the winter solstice.

To prepare for Chinese New Year, people clean their homes and sometimes even redecorate rooms. Food is cooked ahead of time because some Chinese people believe knives should never be used on New Year's Day. You might cut your luck in two! On New Year's Day, people are on their best behavior. Any bad manners, they believe, will continue throughout the year.

The last day of the Chinese New Year celebration is called the Lantern Festival. Lamps made out of red paper are hung everywhere. The highlight of this festival is a parade in which a huge paper dragon weaves its way through the crowds. Some dragons are so long that more than fifty people can dance underneath them. Children follow the dragon, carrying lanterns to light the way and often holding toy dragons.

Make a Chinese Dragon Toy

You will need: pencil ▪ three pieces of red cardstock (13 x 5 inches, 7 x 6 inches, and 8 ½ x 3 inches) ▪ tracing paper ▪ scissors ▪ black felt-tipped pen ▪ gold paint ▪ long strips of red and green cardstock (1 ½ inches and ½ inch wide) ▪ clear tape ▪ glue ▪ two thin sticks ▪ two corks

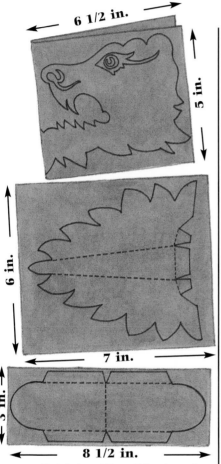

6 ½ in.

5 in.

6 in.

7 in.

3 in.

8 ½ in.

1 Fold the 13- x 5-inch red cardstock in half. Draw the head of a dragon on one side of it, then trace the drawing onto the other side. Draw the shape of a dragon's tail on the 7- x 6-inch piece of cardstock and draw the inside of the dragon's mouth on the 8 ½- x 3-inch piece.

2 Cut out the head and tail and use a black felt-tipped pen and gold paint to decorate them.

3 To make a body, tape one end of a wide strip of red cardstock at a right angle over one end of the same size strip of green cardstock. Fold green over red, then red over green, and so on, to form an accordion. Tape on more red and green cardstock strips to make the body as long as you want it.

4 Fold the tail along the dotted lines. Tuck the flaps into the end of the body and glue them.

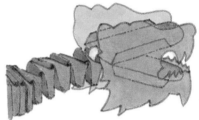

5 Fold the inside of the mouth in half and fold the flaps outward. Tape the mouth inside the head. Tape the body to the head, underneath the mouth.

6 Using two thin strips of red cardstock, make a tongue the same way you made the body. Cut the ends into points. Glue the tongue inside the mouth.

7 Push a stick into each cork. Glue the corks under the head and the tail.

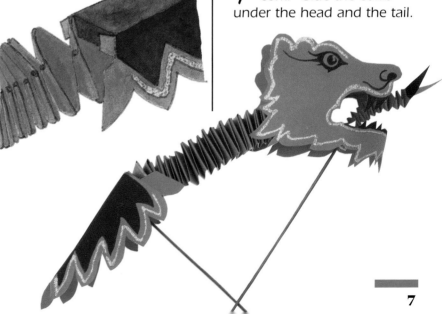

Mardi Gras

The festival known as *Carnival* is a Christian tradition. This celebration is held just before a forty-day period called Lent, during which Christians often fast and make sacrifices in memory of Jesus Christ's suffering and death. The name *carnival* comes from the Latin words meaning "goodbye to meat." Just before this period of sadness and fasting, everyone dances and feasts. In the United States, the annual Carnival celebration is called *Mardi Gras*, which is French for "Fat Tuesday."

In Brazil, dancers practice all year for Mardi Gras, and many people wear specially made costumes and parade through the streets. Some of the costumes are so elaborate that the wearers move around with the parade on a float. In the West Indies, especially in Trinidad, the famous steel bands lead Carnival dancing with calypso music. They play the music on instruments made from used oil drums.

Make Dancing Wings

These wings are painted to look like a butterfly's, but you can make your wings look like a bird's or a moth's or even a bat's — and you can add any design you like!

You will need: tape measure ▪ scissors ▪ old bedsheet or large piece of cotton fabric ▪ needle and thread ▪ two ¹/₂-inch wooden dowels ▪ newspaper ▪ chalk ▪ large and small paintbrushes ▪ red, orange, yellow, and brown inks ▪ gold paint ▪ large safety pin

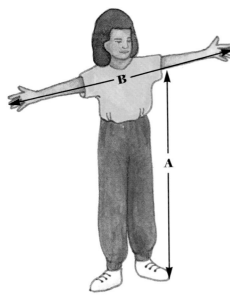

1 Measure yourself from under your arm to the floor (A). Then measure from fingertip to fingertip (B) and add 35 inches. Cut an old bedsheet or a large piece of cotton fabric to these measurements.

2 Sew a narrow hem across the long side of the piece of fabric. Push a dowel through each open end of the hem, then sew the hem openings closed.

3 Spread out the fabric on some newspaper and draw a pattern on it with chalk. Using a large paintbrush and bold strokes, paint over the pattern on the fabric with diluted inks. Begin with red ink, then blend in orange ink. Fill in the background with yellow ink. Make sure the ink soaks through to color both sides of the fabric.

4 Use a small paintbrush to add details in brown ink. When the ink is dry, paint on gold eyes. Cut scallops along the wings' edges.

5 To wear the wings, pin the center of the fabric's hem to the back of your collar. Hold a dowel in each hand to lift the wings up and down.

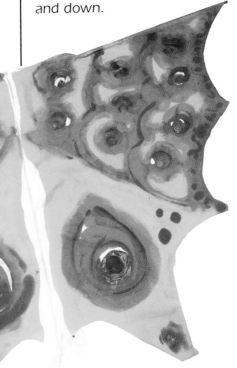

Pakistan

The *Eid* Festivals

Muslims all over the world celebrate two festivals that date back about fourteen hundred years to the time of Islam's founder, the prophet Muhammad. The two festivals are *Eid-ul-Fitr* and *Eid-ul-Adha*.

Eid-ul-Fitr means "the day which returns often." It is held on the day of the new moon at the end of Ramadan. Ramadan is a month–long time of fasting that every devout Muslim observes each year. During Ramadan, no food is eaten between daybreak and sunset. Ramadan ends with the joyful *Eid-ul-Fitr* festival, during which Muslims put on their best clothes and spend time visiting relatives and friends. They also exchange gifts and cards like the ones from Pakistan pictured below. The greeting *Eid Mubarak* means "blessed *Eid*."

Eid-ul-Adha is celebrated throughout the Muslim world at the end of the annual pilgrimage to the Muslim holy city of Mecca. It honors the devotion of the prophet Abraham, who was willing to sacrifice his only son Ismail to Allah (God). Ismail's life was spared when Allah provided a ram to take the boy's place.

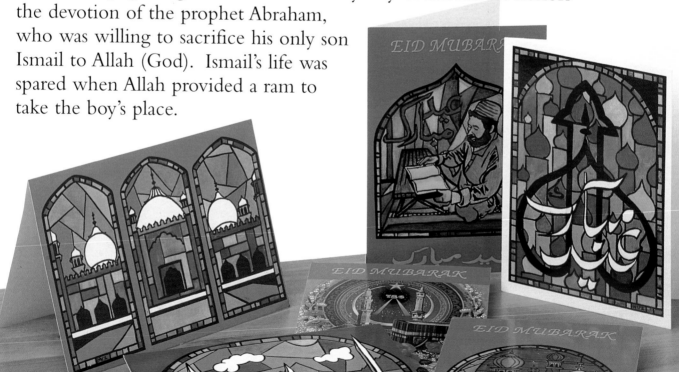

Make an *Eid* Card

You will need: 8- x 8 ½-inch piece of colored cardstock ▪ pencil ▪ tracing paper ▪ 7 ½- x 4-inch piece of wrapping paper ▪ craft knife ▪ glue ▪ gold paint ▪ paintbrush ▪ clear tape ▪ gold foil (from a chocolate bar) ▪ 7 ½- x 8-inch sheet of white paper

عيد مبارك

Use this design or make your own. You could make an envelope out of the same colored cardstock, too.

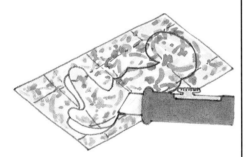

1 Fold the piece of colored cardstock in half. Trace the dotted line around the Arabic writing (above) onto the wrapping paper, then cut along the outline with a craft knife.

2 Glue the wrapping paper to the front of the folded cardstock. Trace the Arabic writing onto the card in the middle of the cut out shape. Cut out the writing with a craft knife. (You could also paint the writing on with gold paint.)

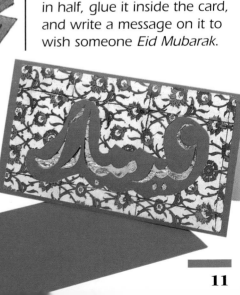

3 Tape gold foil behind the cutout writing to show through the cutout shape. Fold the white paper in half, glue it inside the card, and write a message on it to wish someone *Eid Mubarak.*

Easter

The word "Easter" comes from a pre-Christian celebration honoring Eostre, the goddess of spring. Today, Easter is a Christian celebration commemorating the resurrection of Jesus Christ. Easter also celebrates rebirth and new life.

Eggs, which are a traditional symbol of life, have become an important part of Easter celebrations. In France, on Easter morning, bells ring to tell children it's time to start searching for eggs that have been hidden in the house or the garden. In Germany, children think the Easter rabbit, or bunny, hides the eggs.

Papier-mâché eggs filled with sweets or small gifts are another Easter treat. The art of decorating eggs goes back hundreds of years. Either the eggs are hard-boiled, or the insides are blown out. Then the shells are dyed and decorated. In Ukraine, painting Easter eggs is a popular craft and, possibly, the country's best-known art form. Some of the most elaborately decorated eggs were made by Fabergé, a world-famous Russian jeweler. Every year, he made a beautiful egg to hold the czar's Easter gift to his wife. Today, Fabergé's designs are widely copied for gift eggs.

Make a Fabergé-Style Egg

Filled with chocolates and other sweet treats, this decorated papier-mâché egg makes the perfect Easter gift.

You will need: modeling clay ▪ knife ▪ wooden board (such as a breadboard) ▪ paintbrush ▪ water ▪ paper ▪ white wood glue ▪ scissors ▪ stretchy fabric ▪ strong glue ▪ ribbon ▪ sequins ▪ thin gold cord ▪ thick needle

1 Form a large egg shape out of modeling clay, then cut the shape in half. Place each half, cut side down, on a wooden board.

2 Brush the clay with water and cover each shape with small pieces of wet paper. Brush PVA glue over the layer of paper, then add another layer. Continue adding layers until the paper forms a thick shell. Let the paper shell dry thoroughly.

3 Carefully remove the paper shells from the clay shapes. Trim the edges of the shells with scissors to make them even.

4 Stretch fabric over each shell and glue it around the rim, inside the egg. Glue ribbon over the fabric to make a nice edge.

5 Decorate the outside of each shell by gluing on sequins and gold cord in a pretty pattern.

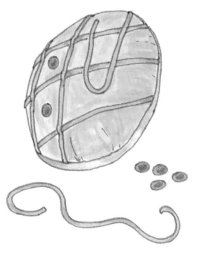

6 Use a thick needle to pierce two holes near the center of each long side on each eggshell. Thread a gold cord through one set of holes in each shell to make a hinge. Thread cord through the holes on the other side of each shell so the egg can be tied closed.

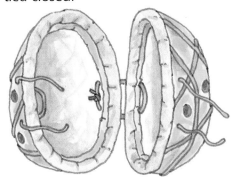

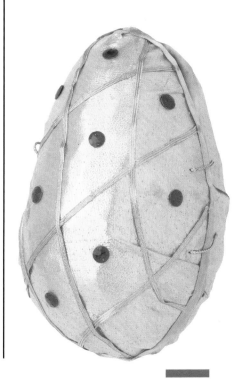

Welcoming Spring

Every country has its own traditional celebrations for the beginning of spring. In India, the Hindu festival of *Holi* begins with a bonfire to celebrate the death of Holika, the demon of winter. On the next day, the fun begins. People throw handfuls of colored powder or spray each other with colored water. The festivities continue with feasting and dancing, when these decorated sticks (below) are used. Then comes *Chaitra*, the first month of spring, when people welcome the New Year with banners and gifts of sweets.

In Christian countries, spring is largely associated with Easter, but ancient pagan festivals remain. Girls dance around the maypole, a tall pole decorated with flowers and ribbons, to encourage the fertility of the crops. The "green man" (above) is an ancient symbol of the links between people and the earth. Some old churches have carvings of the green man, and pubs named "The Green Man" are a reminder of this rural past.

Make a Green Man Mask

Scoring makes cardstock easier to fold, especially along a curved shape. Draw a shape on the cardstock in pencil. Then run the blade of a craft knife gently along the pencil line, piercing the surface of the cardstock but not cutting all the way through it.

You will need: plain cardstock (11 x 15 inches) ▪ pencil ▪ scissors ▪ craft knife ▪ hole punch ▪ thin green ribbon ▪ two sheets of cardstock in different shades of green ▪ clear tape

2 With a craft knife, cut the eyes and mouth. Make slits between the eyes and down the nose. Punch two sets of holes on each side. Thread the ribbon through the holes.

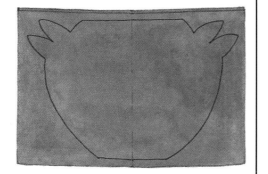

1 Fold the cardstock in half. Draw a mask shape, as shown, and cut it out.

Hold the mask against your face and mark the position of your eyes and mouth with a pencil.

3 Cut eight leaves out of the green cardstock. Score down the lines. Fold the leaves, accordion style, so each one stands out.

4 Cover the mask with leaves. Push the stems through the slits and into the mouth. Tape the stems firmly in place on the back.

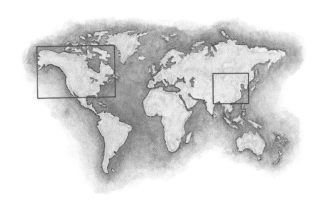

Honoring Ancestors

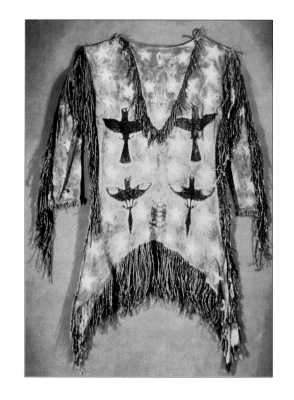

In many cultures, it is important to honor ancestors and to show respect for them. People call on brave heroes and heroines of the past to help them during times of need. When Europeans with guns began their conquest of North America, some Native Americans performed a ghost dance to call upon past warriors for help. They wore special shirts like this one (right).

Chinese people respect their ancestors and send useful articles to their dead relatives. Some of these items are complicated models made out of paper. The models are burned as a way of sending them to the life beyond. A special festival is held at the beginning of winter when cold-weather clothes made from paper, or the money to buy them (below), are burned. The money is of no use on Earth, but it can be cashed at the Bank of Hell!

Make Hell Bank Money

To make your money look like an impressive wad, cut sheets of newspaper to the same size and stack them in a pile. Put one printed bill on the top and one on the bottom. Secure them with a rubber band.

You will need: wooden photo frame ▪ silk or nylon fabric (to fit over frame) ▪ stapler ▪ paper ▪ red and green pencils ▪ two pieces of thin paper ▪ craft knife ▪ newspaper ▪ white paper to print on ▪ pencil ▪ tubes of red and green gouache paint ▪ rubber gloves ▪ short ruler ▪ felt pen

1 To make the screen, stretch the fabric over the back of the frame. Staple it in place.

2 Draw a simple money design in red and green pencil. Trace red areas onto one sheet of thin paper and green areas onto the other sheet. With a craft knife, cut out the traced areas to make two stencils.

3 Spread the newspaper out and place the white paper on top. Lay the red stencil on paper. Mark the edge of the stencil with a pencil.

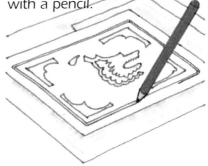

4 Cover the stencil with the screen. Mark the edge of the screen with a pencil.

5 Squeeze red paint onto the screen and draw it over the surface with the ruler. Raise the screen. The stencil should stick to it. Remove the first printed note and let it dry. Repeat as often as the stencil will allow. Remove the screen and the stencil.

6 Wash the screen thoroughly. Lay the second stencil down against the pencil marks. Repeat, using green paint. Use a felt pen to add details to the money.

Everyday Faith

People celebrate their faith on a daily basis by keeping special objects with them or in their homes. In orthodox Christian homes in Russia, a corner of the house is reserved for a shrine with holy pictures, called ikons (below left), on the wall.

Prayer is a universal way in which people communicate with their God or gods. Catholic Christians use a rosary, like this one (below right) from Italy, to help them pray a series of prayers, one bead at a time. Prayer beads are sometimes used by Muslims, Buddhists, and Hindus. The set in the center is called a *chursa* and comes from Tibet.

In Tibet, prayers are often rolled into tall cylinders and placed outside temples. Worshippers turn the cylinders instead of speaking the prayers. This cylinder (right) is a hand-turned version called a prayer wheel. A worshipper swings the cylinder containing the prayers around in a circle. Prayers are also written on long, thin flags so the wind will read them.

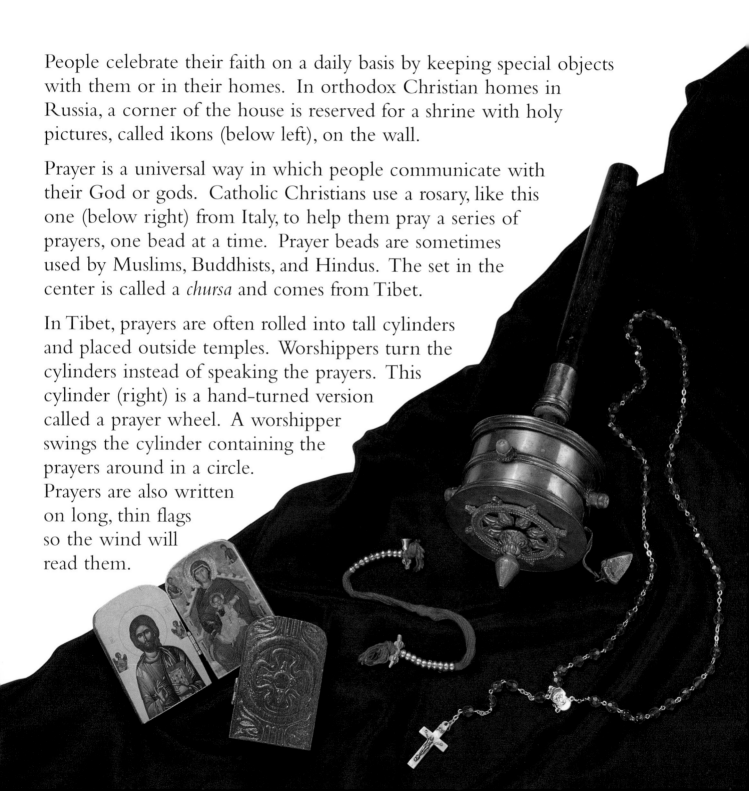

Make a Prayer Wheel

You will need: cardboard mailing tube, about 3 inches wide, with metal or plastic end ▪ thick cardboard ▪ scissors ▪ glue ▪ 40-inch bamboo stick ▪ two corks ▪ cardboard tube, 1 x 9 inches ▪ self-hardening modeling clay ▪ thin gold cord ▪ decorative button ▪ gold paint ▪ gold braid ▪ glue ▪ plastic "jewels" ▪ varnish ▪ paper ▪ pencil

1 To make the drum, cut 2.75 inches from the end of the cardboard tube. Make a lid by cutting out a disk of cardboard just a little bigger than the tube. Cut another disk slightly smaller than the inside of the tube. Glue the disks together.

2 Make a handle by pushing the stick into a cork. Push the cork into the small cardboard tube.

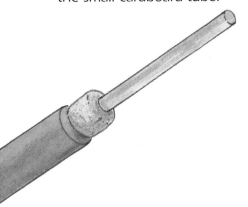

3 Mold a weight from clay. Make a hole in the weight. Pierce two holes in the side of the drum. Thread the cord through the drum holes and the weight. Tie it on the inside of the drum.

4 To assemble the drum, pierce a hole in the base and the lid. Fit the lid onto the drum. Push the stick through both holes in the drum. Make sure the drum turns freely.

5 Push the second cork onto the end of the stick and glue the button on top. Paint it gold. Glue on the gold braid and "jewels." Varnish it.

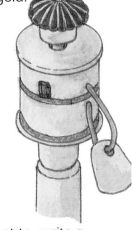

6 If you want to, write a prayer on a long, thin piece of paper. Roll it up and place it inside the drum. Swing the weight around to turn the prayer wheel.

Harvest Festivals

People who live in cities may have lost contact with the yearly harvest of crops, yet festivals are still held to remind us how important these events are. In Israel, there are three harvests: in spring, summer, and autumn. This market in Jerusalem (right) has been set up for the September harvest festival of *Sukkot*.

Thanksgiving Day in the United States dates back to the time when the first settlers from England celebrated their survival during the first year in their new country. Families and friends gather for a meal of turkey, corn, pumpkins, cranberries, and sweet potatoes — the foods that the Native Americans taught the settlers to raise.

In the United Kingdom, harvest festivals are mostly celebrated in Christian churches. An old tradition is to bake a loaf in the shape of a sheaf of wheat (left), using the last of the harvested grain. The loaf is taken to the richly decorated church as a symbol of thanksgiving for the harvest.

Make Harvest Paperweights

These little loaves make good gifts. Write the person's name in the band across the middle before you bake them. If you prefer to make loaves that you can eat, use bread dough instead of salt dough and follow a recipe for making bread.

You will need: 1 cup plain flour ▪ 1 cup salt ▪ bowl ▪ water ▪ fork ▪ wooden board ▪ blunt knife ▪ oven ▪ varnish ▪ brush

1 Mix the flour and salt in a bowl. Add water slowly, mixing with a fork, until a firm dough is formed.

2 Pull off a hand-sized lump and roll it into a ball on the board. Press it with your hand to form an oblong shape.

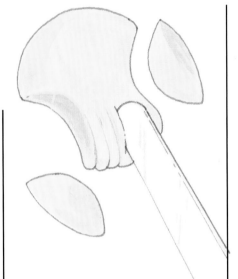

3 With a blunt knife, cut away the sides of the dough to form the wheat sheaf shape. Cut stalk lines in the bottom half.

4 With more dough, make a long, thin roll. Break off small pieces and roll the ends into points. Press these into the top half, in diagonal rows, to form wheat grains. Lay a flat piece of dough around the middle of the sheaf.

5 Leave the dough to rise a little. Bake it in a medium-hot oven until it is as hard as a biscuit. Varnish it when it cools.

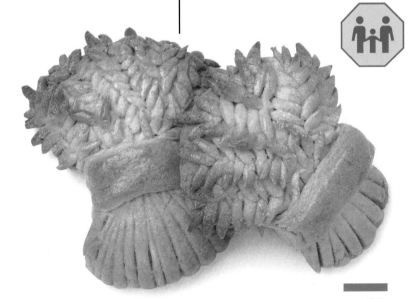

Halloween and All Souls' Day

The period from October 31st to November 2nd is celebrated by many Christians as the time to remember those who have died. All Hallows Eve, or Halloween, has become associated with ghosts and spirits who come back to haunt the living.

In Mexico, All Souls' Day is celebrated as the Day of the Dead, when people visit the graves of their relatives, often singing, dancing, and feasting there. Days are spent preparing for this fiesta. Sugar model making dates back over one hundred years and has developed into a remarkable skill. Elaborate skeletons and skulls (above), coffins, saints, and animals are made for children to enjoy. They are formed in hollow shapes out of hard white sugar and decorated with bright colors.

In North America and parts of Europe, a traditional symbol of this season is the pumpkin head. The pumpkin is hollowed out, carved with a scary face, and used as a lantern. (All the visiting spirits must leave the Earth again by All Saints' Day on November 1st.) The North American tradition of "trick or treat" comes from the idea that people must be kind to dead ancestors to prevent them from playing tricks.

Make a Sugar Skull

You will need: premade white icing or fondant icing ▪ wooden board ▪ round-bladed knife or modeling tool ▪ food coloring ▪ brush ▪ cake decorations

This skull is not hollowed out in the same way as a Mexican sugar skull but made from premade icing, which is easier to use. It will be very sweet to eat all at once, so make your skulls small or share them with lots of people!

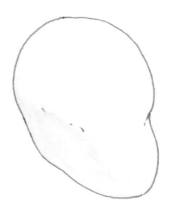

4 Let the icing sugar harden. Paint the features with food coloring. Decorate with cake decorations.

2 At the narrower end, squash in the sides to form cheekbones.

3 Use both ends of the knife or modeling tool to form the features. Halfway down, press in the eye sockets. Below these, form two nostril holes. Make teeth shapes along the bottom of the jaw.

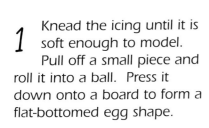

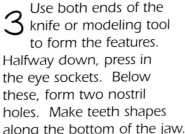

1 Knead the icing until it is soft enough to model. Pull off a small piece and roll it into a ball. Press it down onto a board to form a flat-bottomed egg shape.

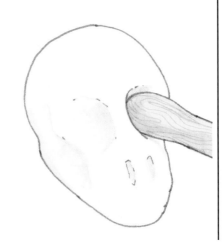

Founder's Days

Most religions hold festivals in honor of their founders. *Wesak* is the Mahayana Buddhists' celebration of the life of Buddha. Wesak falls on the full moon in April or May. The Buddha's birth, his first steps, his enlightenment under a bodhi tree, and his entry into *nirvana* are all commemorated. Cards like these (below) are exchanged during the festival.

In India, Sikhs celebrate the births of their founder, the guru Nanak, and of nine other important gurus. The main part of these celebrations is the Akhand Path, which is a continuous, three-day reading of the Adi Granth, the Sikh scriptures. Special garlands are worn or draped over the portraits of the gurus as a sign of respect. The design in the center of the one below is the Sikh symbol *ek onkar*.

Make a Portrait Garland

This garland has a picture of guru Nanak in the center. You can use the same method to make a garland celebrating any festival that is important to you.

You will need: pencil ▪ thin cardboard, 7 x 8 inches ▪ glue ▪ picture or postcard ▪ scissors ▪ needle and thread ▪ 1¹/₂ yards gold tinsel ▪ pins ▪ 3 yards red ribbon, 1 inch wide ▪ 1 yard gold giftwrap ribbon ▪ 14 inches thin ribbon

1 Draw a shield shape on the cardboard. Glue the picture in the middle. Cut out the shield.

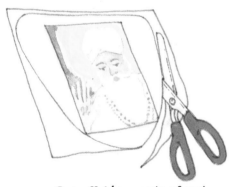

2 Cut off 1¹/₂ yards of red ribbon. Sew a running stitch along the center. Pull the thread to gather the ribbon so that it fits around the shield.

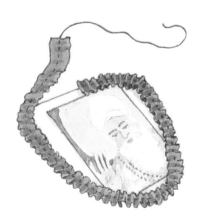

3 Cut enough tinsel to edge the shield and lay it on the cardboard. Pin it in place. Lay the gathered ribbon on top and pin through the tinsel. Sew through all the layers to hold them in place. Remove the pins.

4 Cut two 15-inch lengths each of tinsel, red ribbon, and gold ribbon. Make two straps by sewing the red ribbon to the gold. Sew the tinsel down the middle.

5 Sew the straps to the top of the shield. Sew the thin ribbon to the ends of the straps to complete the garland.

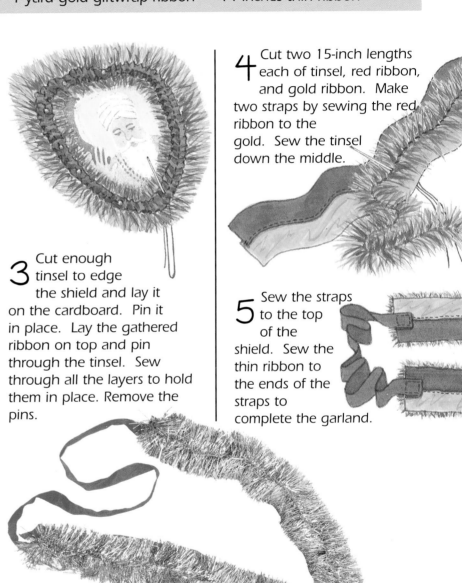

Festivals of Light

In India, *Diwali* is the major Hindu festival. The name comes from *deepawali*, which means "a row of lights." It marks the beginning of the New Year for many people in India. The festival lasts for several days, with fireworks and parties. Little clay lamps (lower left) are made and set in rows in windows to mark the return from banishment of Rama and Sita, the hero and heroine of the Indian sacred text, *Ramayana*.

The Jewish festival of lights is called *Chanukah*. It commemorates the relighting of the *menorah*, the candlestick in the temple at Jerusalem in 168 B.C. At that time, the oil for the temple lamps miraculously burned for eight days. The festival lasts for the same length of time. During the festival, one of the eight candles on the candlestick (right), is lit every day. The ninth candle is used to light the others. Parties are held, special food is served, and children play a game with a spinning top called a dreidel (below center). The top has four sides, each with a Hebrew letter that stands for the words "a great miracle happened here."

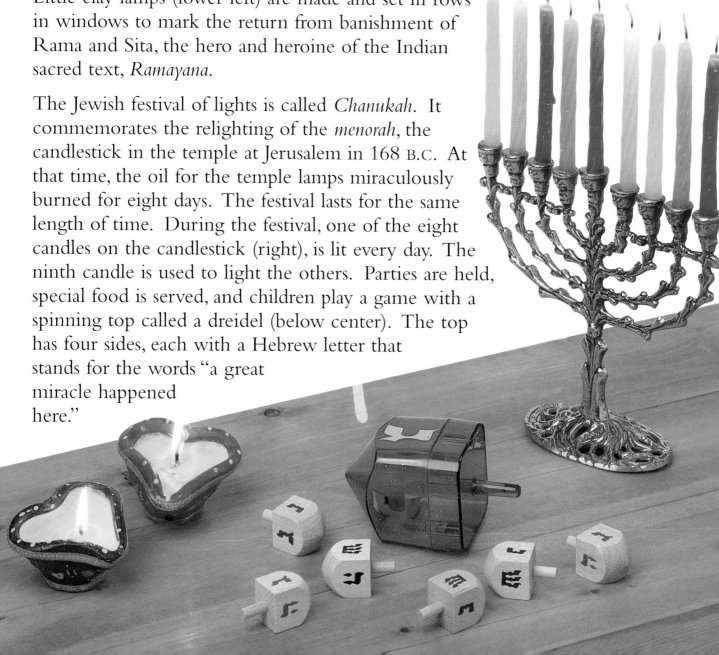

Make Diwali Lights

You will need: modeling clay ▪ small candles ▪ blunt knife ▪ poster paints ▪ brush ▪ varnish ▪ thin gold cord ▪ glue ▪ sequins

1 Pull off a piece of clay the size of a golf ball. Roll it into a ball. Push your thumb into the center. Pinch and turn the clay to make a small thumb pot.

2 Press the walls of the pot thinner until you can fit a candle in the bottom.

3 Mold the pot into a heart shape around the candle. Trim the top of the rim flat.

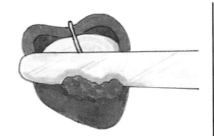

4 Roll out a thin roll of clay. Lay it around the edge of the pot. Let it dry hard.

5 Paint the inside and outside of the pot in bright colors. Decorate it with dots and dashes.

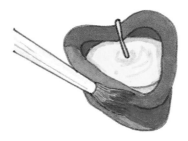

6 Varnish the pot for a shiny finish. Glue the cord around the top and base. Glue sequins around the middle.

Christmas

In Roman times, the winter solstice was celebrated with a feast in honor of the god Saturn. When the Romans adopted Christianity, the Christ Mass (Christmas), which commemorated the birth of Jesus, took over from this popular festival. Many traditions surround the celebration of Christmas. Families get together, eat a special meal, and give each other presents. Christians attend special services at church, where there is often a crib or nativity scene. The carved, wooden nativity scene (lower right) comes from southern India. The stable scene behind it is from Nigeria.

In Peru, *retablos* with nativity scenes inside are popular. When Christianity was first taken to South America, traveling priests carried small altars with them for festivals. These altars gradually developed into portable boxes decorated with saints and scenes from everyday life. Today, Christmas retablos like the ones shown here (below left) show Mary, Joseph, and Jesus with local people gathered around.

Make a Retablo Scene

This retablo would make a lovely centerpiece for Christmas. You could also make one showing scenes from your own surroundings. You could even add characters representing your family or friends.

You will need: large sheet of corrugated cardboard ▪ pencil ▪ craft knife ▪ masking tape ▪ two thin oblong boxes (such as boxes from toothpaste and canned tomatoes) ▪ strong glue ▪ two strips of cotton fabric ▪ water ▪ paper ▪ white wood glue ▪ brush ▪ poster paints ▪ modeling clay or potato dough (see page 5) ▪ flat board ▪ varnish

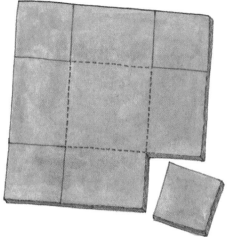

1 Draw the box pattern on the cardboard. With a craft knife, cut around the edges and score along the dotted lines.

Fold the cardboard into a box. Tape the sides.

2 Cut out two pieces for doors and a triangle for the top. Cut the oblong boxes to fit. Put them inside as steps.

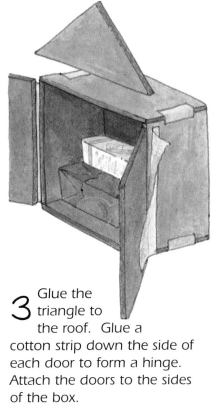

3 Glue the triangle to the roof. Glue a cotton strip down the side of each door to form a hinge. Attach the doors to the sides of the box.

4 Cover the whole box with a layer of papier-mâché (see page 13). Paint the inside dark blue and green and the outside white. Decorate the outside.

5 Use clay or potato dough to make the model figures. Work on a flat board. Let the figures dry. Paint them with poster paints. Varnish them for a glossy finish.

6 Glue the figures in position. Group the shepherds and the kings together. Face them in opposite directions. Baby Jesus should face forward.

Glossary

Allah: the Arabic word for God

ancestor: a past member of a family

banishment: removal from a state or country

calypso: a West Indian song that usually comments on local events

commemorate: to celebrate in memory of someone or something

cylinders: tubes

czar: the name given to the rulers of Russia in the past

elaborate: complex, detailed, or ornate

enlightenment: a sudden moment of understanding or seeing the truth about something

fast: to go without food

fertility: the ability to produce good crops for the harvest

festivity: a celebration

fiesta: a religious festival held in Spanish-speaking countries

founder: a person who starts an organization or leads a group of believers

garland: a circle of flowers or plants that is used for decoration

guru: a religious teacher or leader of the Hindu religion

hallow: to make holy

harvest: the season for gathering crops

ikon: a picture that is made to be used in worship

maypole: a tall pole decorated with flowers and ribbons. It is the centerpiece of special dances in some countries during May

nativity: birth, especially the birth of Jesus

nirvana: in the Buddhist religion, a feeling of perfect peace and of being blessed

orthodox: strict and traditional

reaping: cutting and gathering a crop

replica: an exact copy of something

resurrection: the return back to life after dying

retablo: a portable altar that consists of a box-shaped frame with decorated panels

ritual: a religious or very serious set of actions

sacrifices: things that are given up for a belief or an end

sheaf: a bunch of stalks of a cereal or other plant material bound together

solstice: the beginning of summer or the beginning of winter

temperate: describes areas of the world with a mild climate

tradition: information, beliefs, or customs handed down from one generation to the next

More Books to Read

Christmas Crafts from Around the World. Judy Ann Sadler (Kids Can Press)

Festival Decorations. Anne Civardi, Penny King (Crabtree)

Holiday Origami. Jill Smolinski (McGraw–Hill)

Traditional Crafts from China. Culture Crafts (series). Florence Temko (Lerner)

The World of Holidays. Life Around the World (series). Paula S. Wallace (Gareth Stevens)

Web Sites

Chinese New Year
www.educ.uvic.ca/faculty/mroth/438/ CHINA/chinese_new_year.html

The Day of the Dead
www.public.iastate.edu/~rjsalvad/scmfaq/ muertos.html

Sukkot
www.cstone.net/~bry-back/ holidayfun/sukkot.html

Christmas in Sweden
www.algonet.se/~bernadot/christmas/14.html

Index

All Souls' Day 22
ancestors 16, 22

Brazil 8
Buddha 24

Carnival 8
Chanukah 26
China 6, 16
Chinese New Year 6
Christmas 28

Day of the Dead 22
Diwali 26
Diwali lights 27
dough recipes 5
dragon 6, 7
dreidel (spinning top) 26

Easter 12, 14
eggs, decorated 12, 13
Eid card (greeting
    card) 11
Eid festivals 10
Europe 14

festival crafts kit 5

Germany 12
ghost dance 16
green man 14
green man mask 15

Halloween 22
harvest festivals 4, 20
harvest loaf
    paperweights 21
Hell Bank money 16, 17
Holi 14

ikons 18

India 14, 24, 26, 28
Israel 20, 26
Italy 18

Jewish festival 26

Lantern Festival 6
Lent 8
light, festivals of 4, 26

Mardi Gras 8
maypole 14
Mexico 22
Muslim festivals 10
Myanmar 24

nativity scenes 28, 29
Nigeria 28
North America 16, 22

pagan festivals 14
Pakistan 10
paper money 16, 17
papier-mâché 12, 29
Peru 28
portrait garland 24, 25
prayer beads 18
prayer wheel 18, 19
pumpkin head 22

Ramadan 10
religious festivals 4, 10,
    12, 22, 24, 26, 28
retablo 28, 29
rosary 18
Russia 12, 18

seasonal festivals 4, 14
Sikh festival 24
spring festivals 14
steel bands 8

sugar model making
    22, 23
sugar skull 23
Sukkot 20

Thanksgiving Day 20
Tibet 18
"trick or treat" 22
Trinidad 8

Ukraine 12
United Kingdom 20
United States 8, 20

Wesak 24
wings, dancing 9